Let's All Sing
The Beatles

Collection of Favorites for Young Voices

Arrangements by Roger Emerson and Mac Huff

T0079158

Table of Contents

HAL•LEONARD®
CORPORATION

7777 W. BLUEMOUND RD. P.O. BOX 13819 MILWAUKEE, WI 53213

Visit Hal Leonard Online at
www.halleonard.com

Can't Buy Me Love

Words and Music by
JOHN LENNON and PAUL McCARTNEY
Arranged by MAC HUFF

ev - 'ry-bod - y tells me so.___ Can't buy me love___ love,___

no, no, no,___ no!

Say you don't need no dia - mond rings___ and I'll be sat - is - fied.___

Tell me that you want the kind___ of things___ that mon - ey just can't buy.___

mon - ey just can't buy.___ I don't care too much for mon - ey,

mon - ey can't buy me love. Can't buy me love, ___ love, ___

love, ___ love. ___ Can't buy me love, ___ love, ___

love. ___

Drive My Car

Words and Music by
JOHN LENNON and PAUL McCARTNEY
Arranged by ROGER EMERSON

Moderate rock (♩ = 112)

Beep, beep, mm beep, beep.   Beep, beep, mm beep, beep.   Yeah!

Asked a girl   what she want-ed to be.___   She said, "Ba-by,

can't you   see?___   I wan-na be fa-mous,   a star of the screen,___   but

DO NOT
PHOTOCOPY

Ba - by, you can drive my car,_____ and may - be I'll love_____ you."

Beep, beep, mm beep, beep. Yeah!_____ Beep, beep, mm beep, beep. Yeah! __

__ Beep, beep, mm beep, beep. Yeah!_____

Beep, beep, mm beep, beep. Beep, beep, mm beep, beep. Yeah!_____

A Hard Day's Night

Words and Music by
JOHN LENNON and PAUL McCARTNEY
Arranged by ROGER EMERSON

I should be sleep-in'_____ like a log._____ So why I

love to come home, 'cause when I get you a-lone, you know I feel_____ al - right._____

You know I feel_____ al - right._____ You know I

feel al - right._____ Feel al - right.

Here Comes the Sun

Words and Music by
GEORGE HARRISON
Arranged by MAC HUFF

Octopus' Garden

Words and Music by JOHN LENNON,
PAUL McCARTNEY and RICHARD STARKEY
Arranged by ROGER EMERSON

DO NOT
PHOTOCOPY

Oct - o - pus - 's Gar - den in the shade.

lit - tle hide - a - way_____ be - neath the waves.__

G   A

He'd let us in;___ knows where we've been__ in his

Rest - ing our head___ on the sea - bed,___ in an

D   Bm

Oct - o - pus - 's Gar - den in the shade.

Oct - o - pus - 's Gar - den near a cave.

G   A